Ballet

Car… …laisted

OXFORD
UNIVERSITY PRESS

Contents

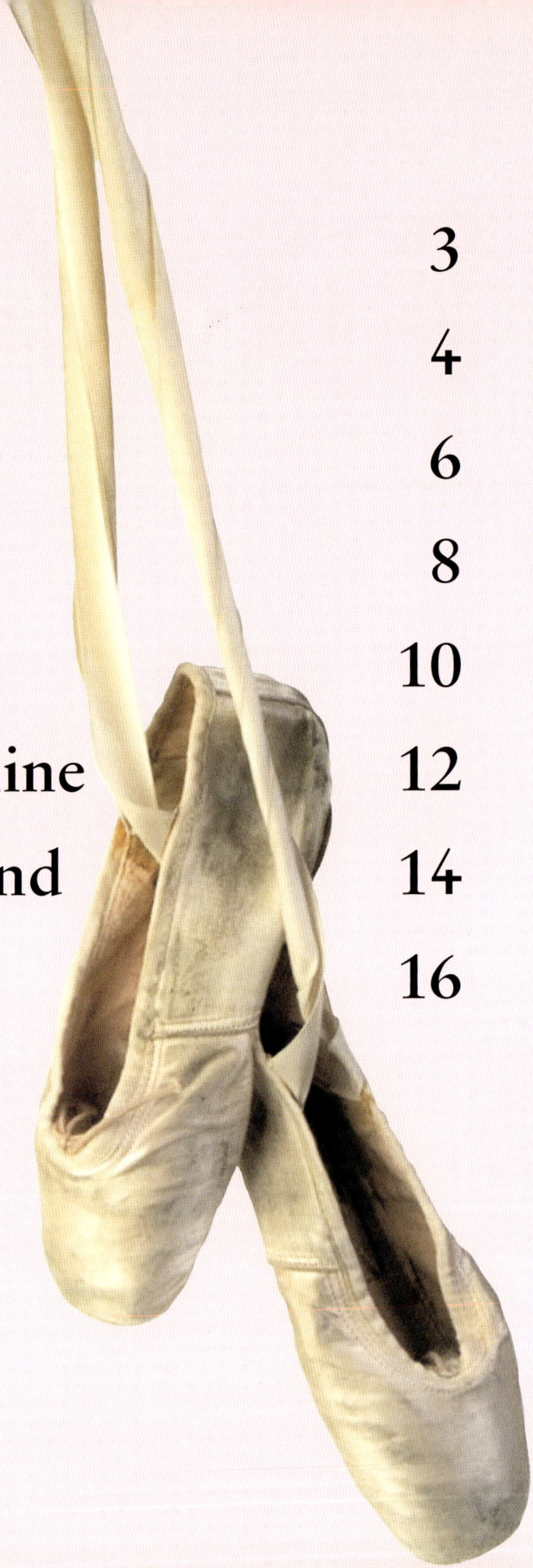

Introduction

On Mondays we go to our ballet class.

Stretching

First, we sit on the floor.

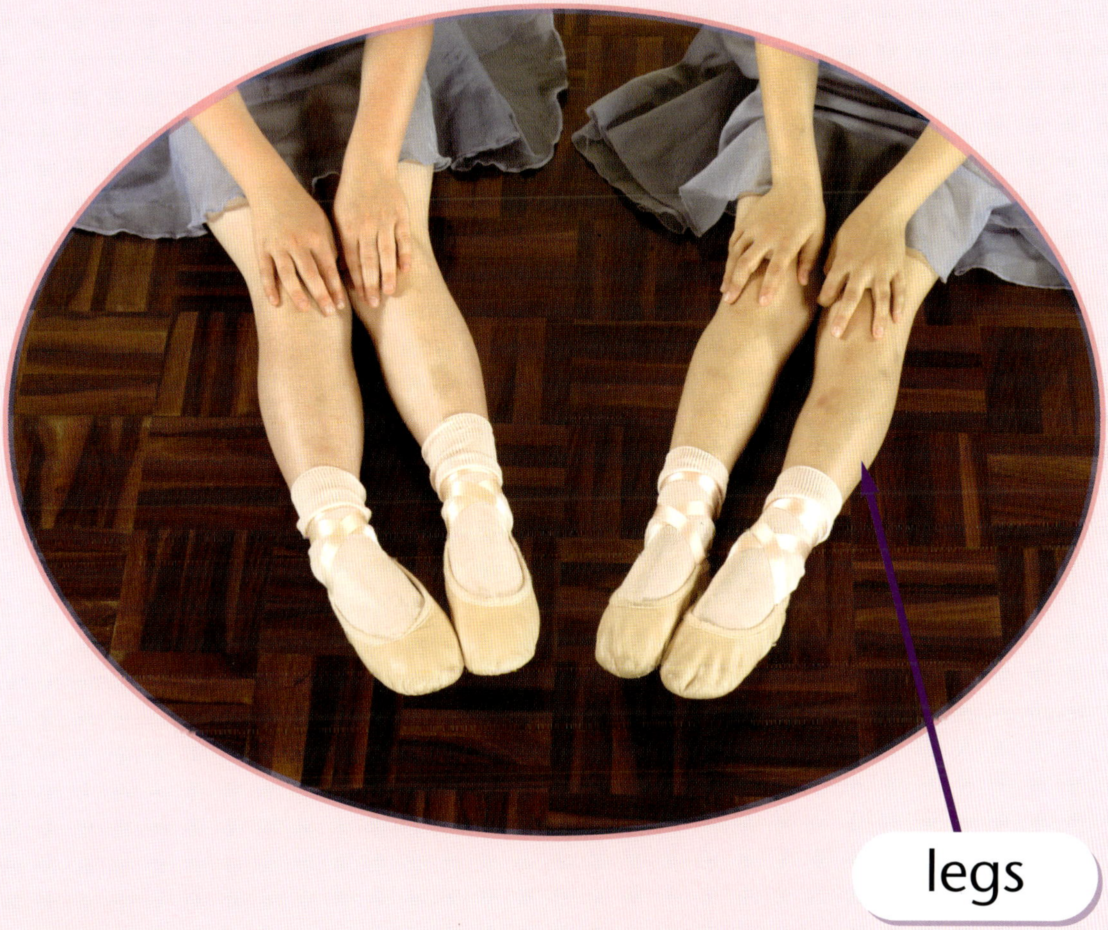

We stretch out our legs in front.

Bending

We stand up to do knee bends.

I bend down to the music.
Then I pull myself up again.

Jumping

I love to jump in my ballet class.
I go up and down to the music.

I point my toes when I go up.

Skipping

Then we skip across the room.

I go first.

Dancing in a line

Next we all dance in a line.
We all hold hands.

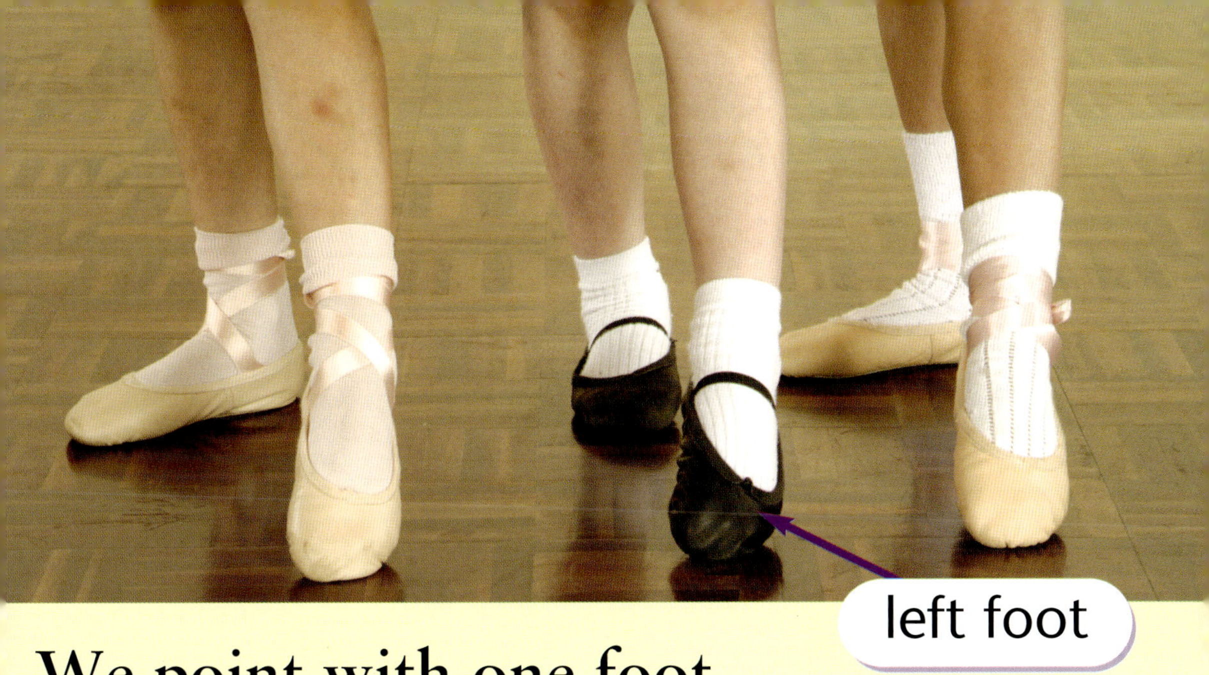

We point with one foot.

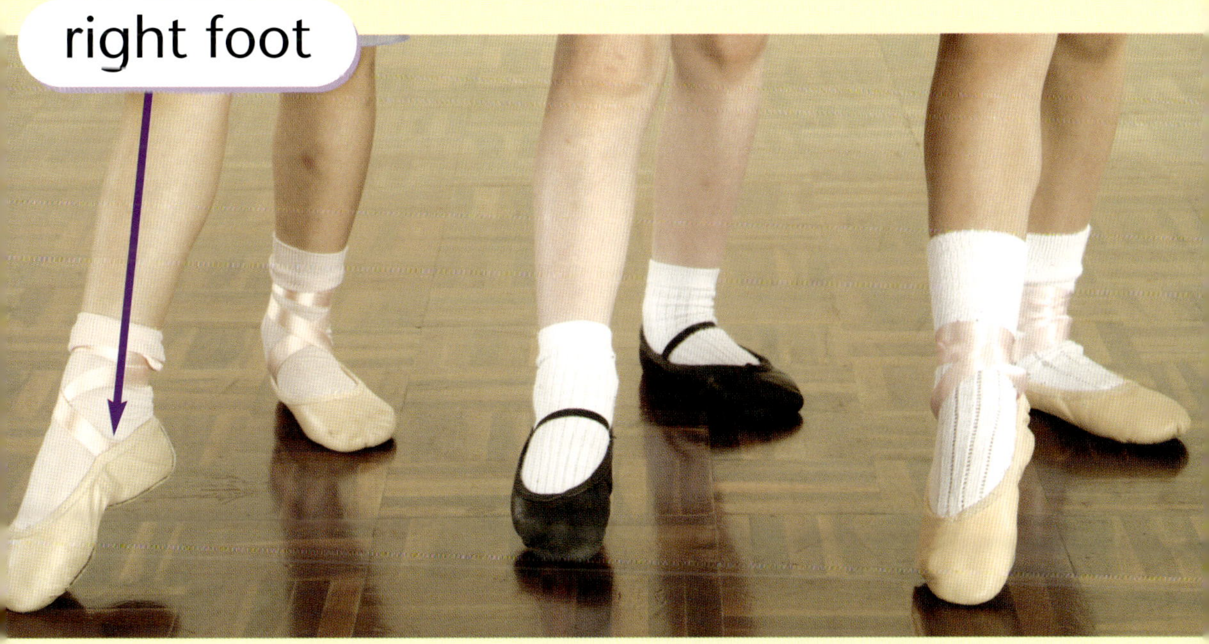

Then we point with the other foot.

Dancing around

We swirl and twirl to the music.

I love to dance at my ballet class.

Index